My First Book of Planets

ALL ABOUT THE SOLAR SYSTEM FOR KIDS

BRUCE BETTS, PHD

ROCKRIDGE PRESS

For general information on our other products and services or to obtain technical support, please contact our Customer Care Department within the United States at (866) 744-2665, or outside the United States at (510) 253-0500.

Rockridge Press publishes its books in a variety of electronic and print formats. Some content that appears in print may not be available in electronic books, and vice versa.

Interior & Cover Designer: Sean Doyle
Art Producer: Tom Hood
Editor: Laura Bryn Sisson
Production Editor: Rachel Taenzler

ISBN: Print 978-1-64611-836-6 | eBook 978-1-64611-837-3
R1
Printed in China

For my sons, KEVIN and DANIEL

Artist's drawing

The Solar System

You live on a **planet** named Earth. Earth goes around the Sun, and the path it takes is called an **orbit**.

Earth is part of the **solar system**. The solar system has the Sun in the middle and lots of big things that go around the Sun.

Planets are big, ball-shaped objects that move around the Sun. Our solar system has eight planets.

The four planets closest to the Sun have rocks and ground you could stand on. Those planets are Mercury, Venus, Earth, and Mars.

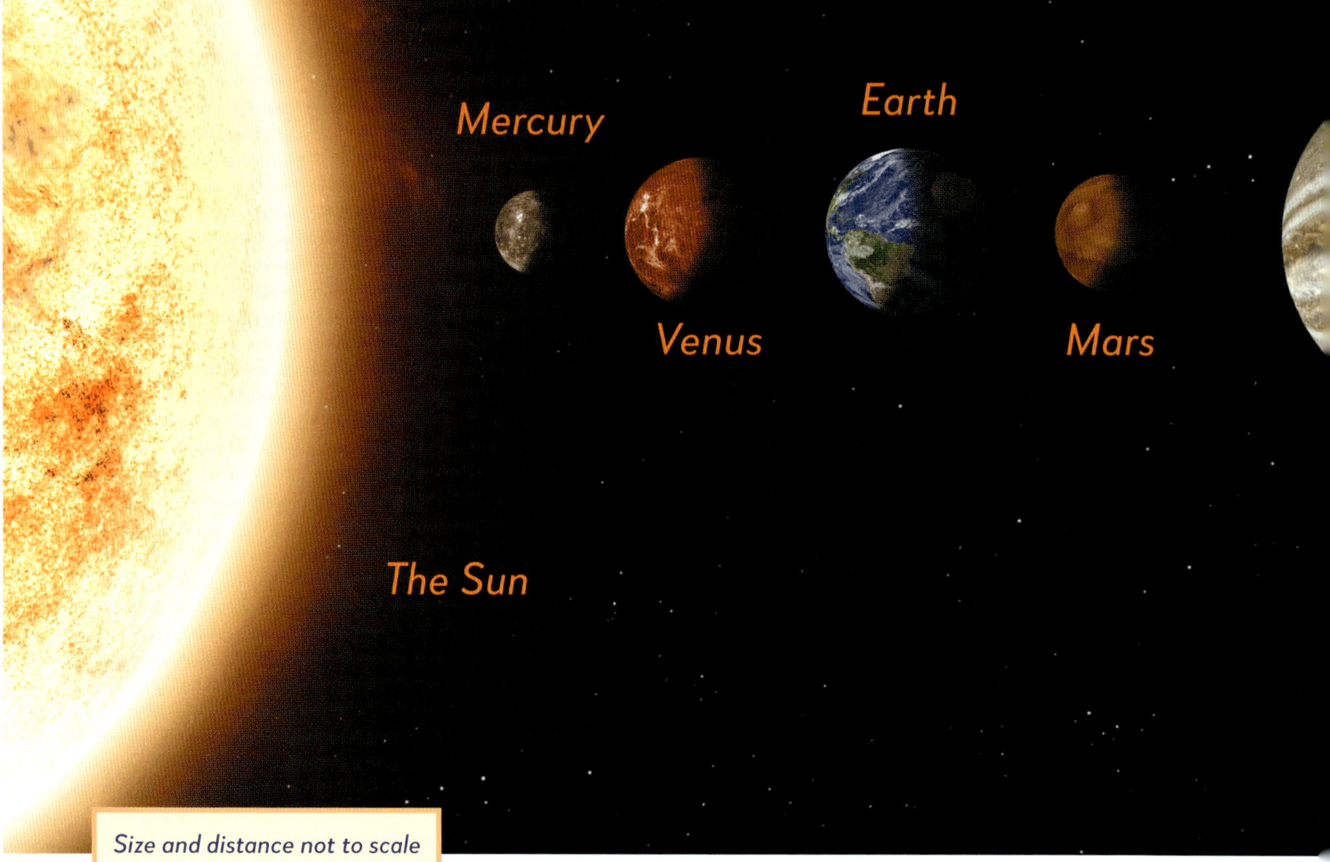

Size and distance not to scale

The four planets farthest from the Sun are much bigger and called **giant planets**. They are mostly made of **gas**, like what fills a balloon, so you couldn't stand on them. Those planets are Jupiter, Saturn, Uranus, and Neptune.

The Sun

The Sun is a **star**. A star is a huge ball of hot, glowing gas. There are many stars. You can see some in the night sky. Stars are much hotter than fire.

The Sun is our star, and it is very special. It is the only star close enough to keep us warm and give us lots of light.

WARNING: NEVER STARE AT THE SUN.
YOU CAN HURT YOUR EYES.

Artist's drawing

The Sun is gigantic. One million Earths could fit inside the Sun. The size of Earth compared to the Sun is like the size of a mouse compared to an elephant.

The distance from the Earth to the Sun is about 150 million kilometers, or 93 million miles. That's really far! In this book, we will say how far other planets are from the Sun by using the distance between Earth and the Sun.

*A **day** is the time it takes a planet to spin all the way around once.*
*A **year** is the time it takes a planet to go all the way around the Sun.*

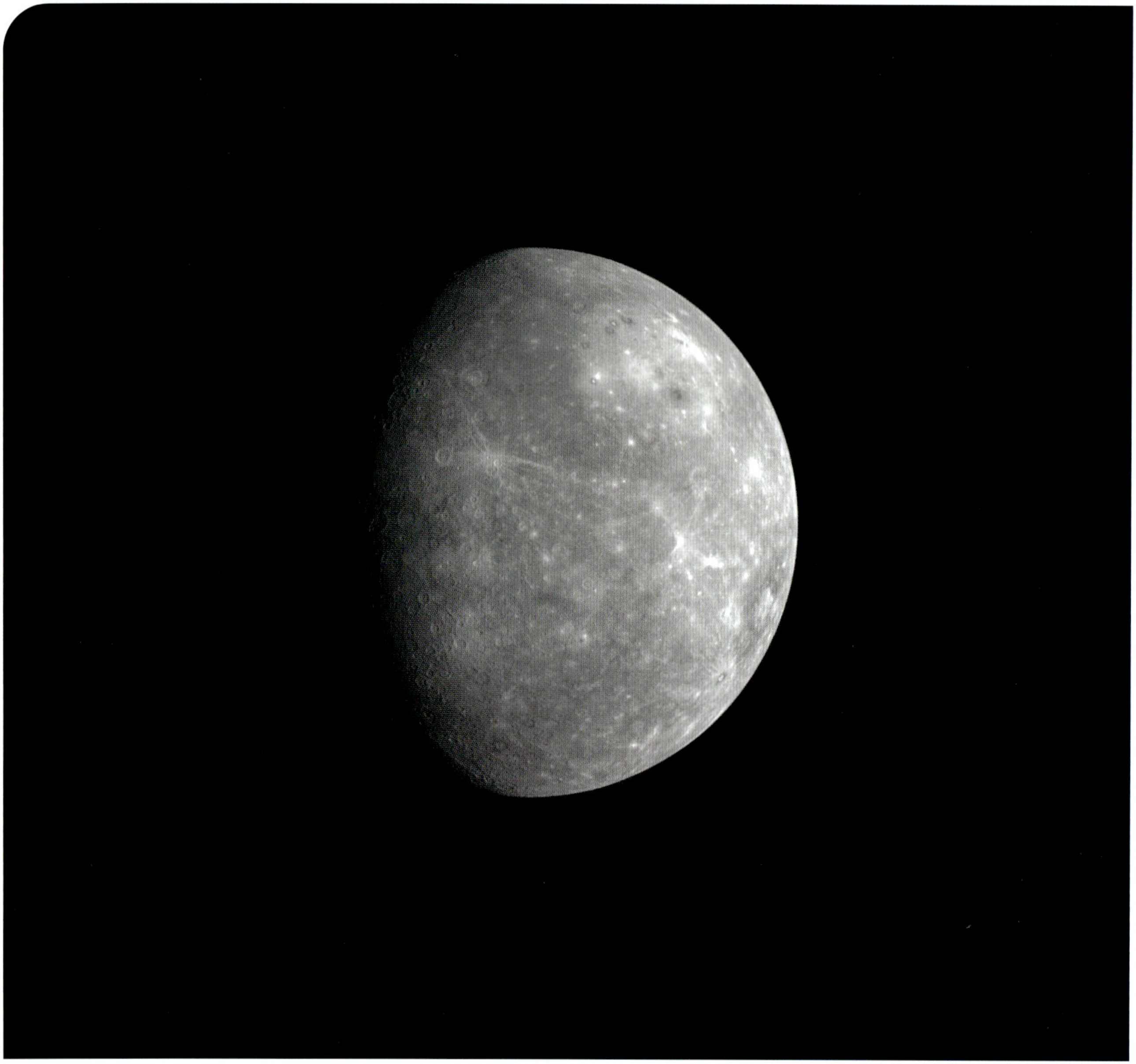

Mercury

Mercury is the closest planet to the Sun and the smallest. It is a rocky planet and mostly gray in color.

Mercury has almost no **atmosphere**, the gas that can surround a planet. An atmosphere lets people, animals, and plants breathe. But there is nothing to breathe on Mercury.

In the daytime, the ground on Mercury is hotter than an oven. At nighttime, it is much colder than a freezer.

Sometimes, you can see Mercury in our night sky. It looks like a bright star.

How Big? Almost 18 Mercurys could fit inside Earth

How Far from the Sun? A little less than ½ the Earth-to-Sun distance

How Many Moons? Zero

Mercury is covered with **impact craters** that look like bowls. When a rock flies through space really fast and hits the ground, it makes a crater.

Venus

Venus is the second planet from the Sun. It is a little smaller than Earth. It has a solid, rocky surface (or ground).

Venus spins the opposite way compared to Earth.

Venus has an atmosphere that keeps it warm like a blanket. The ground is very hot. It stays hot all day and night.

The surface of Venus is hotter than a stove.

Venus has lots of clouds. If you stood on Venus, you would not be able to see the Sun because of the clouds.

Sometimes you can see Venus in our night sky. It looks like the brightest star in the sky.

The bubbles in soda are the same gas that makes up a lot of the atmosphere on Venus.

How Big? A little smaller than Earth

How Far from the Sun? A little more than ½ the Earth-to-Sun distance

How Many Moons? Zero

Earth

Earth is the third planet from the Sun. It is our planet and our home. We live on the biggest of the four rocky planets.

For Earth, one orbit around the Sun takes one year. How old are you? That is how many times you have traveled around the Sun.

Earth is mostly covered with oceans. From space, Earth looks very blue because of the oceans and white because of clouds.

Earth is special. It is the only place we know of that has life. Life on Earth includes plants and animals. Life on Earth includes you!

You need to drink water. All living things need water. Earth is the only place in the solar system with water ready for you to drink. That makes Earth perfect for life.

How Big? About 8,000 miles across

How Far from the Sun? 93 million miles

How Many Moons? 1

The Moon

A **moon** is an object in space that goes around a bigger object, like a planet. Some planets have many moons, and some have none. Earth has one moon, and we call it the Moon.

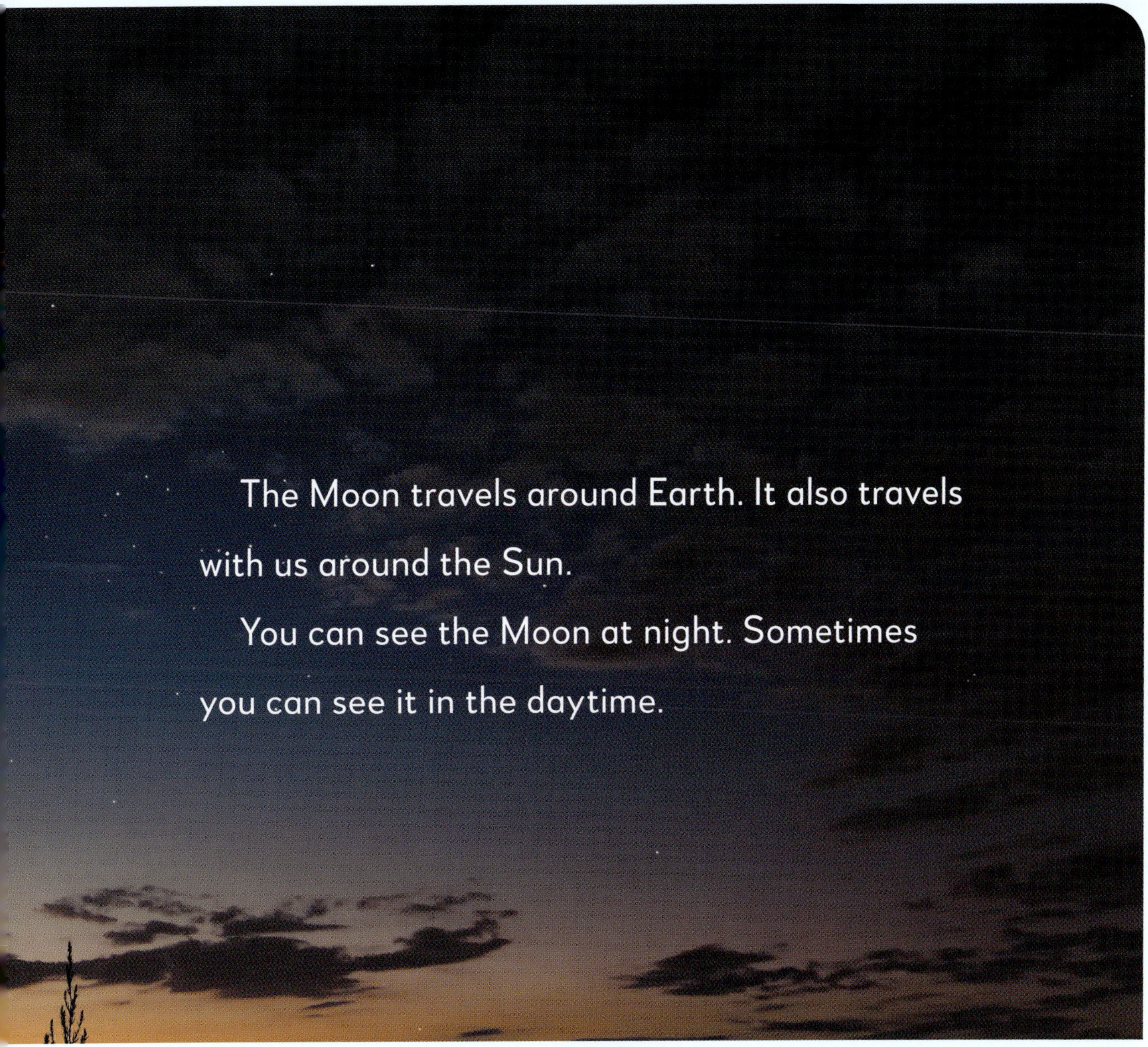

The Moon travels around Earth. It also travels with us around the Sun.

You can see the Moon at night. Sometimes you can see it in the daytime.

From Earth, we always see the same side of the Moon. Sometimes we see all of it lit up by sunlight. That is called a full moon. Other times we see part of the Moon lit up and part of it dark. The lit part is in daytime on the Moon, and the dark part is in nighttime on the Moon.

If you think of the Moon as a tennis ball, then Earth would be a little bigger than a basketball.

People have walked on only two places in our solar system: Earth and the Moon.

Mars

Mars is the fourth planet from the Sun. It is called the Red Planet. Red rocks and dust cover its surface.

A long time ago, there were seas and flowing water on Mars. Now it has some ice (solid water) but no liquid water you could drink at its surface. Mars is much colder than Earth.

Earth has icy polar caps. Mars does, too. Polar caps are big areas of ice on the top or bottom of a planet. They look like big white spots.

Mars looks like a desert does on Earth. It has mountains, canyons, sand dunes, and plains.

How Big? Almost 7 Mars could fit inside Earth

How Far from the Sun? About 1½ Earth-to-Sun distances

How Many Moons? 2

Lots of robot **spacecraft** are studying Mars. Spacecraft are vehicles that can travel outside of Earth. Some are in orbit around Mars. Others look like weird, small cars and drive on the surface.

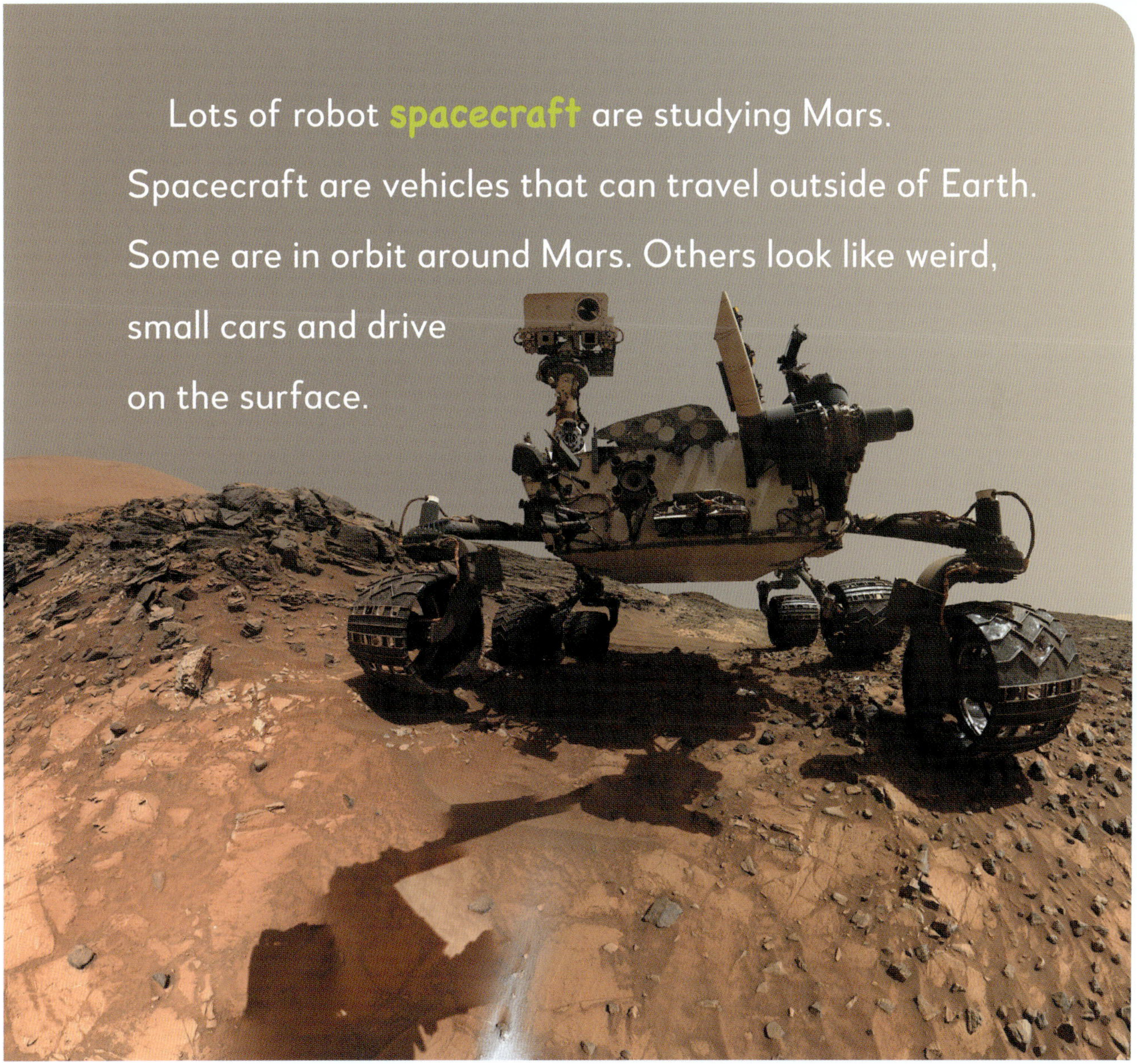

The Asteroid Belt

An **asteroid** is a small object in space made of rock or metal. Well, it is small compared to a planet. It is big compared to you or me!

The asteroid belt has millions of asteroids orbiting the Sun. That's a lot of asteroids! Even so, the asteroid belt is so big that most of it is empty space.

Artist's drawing

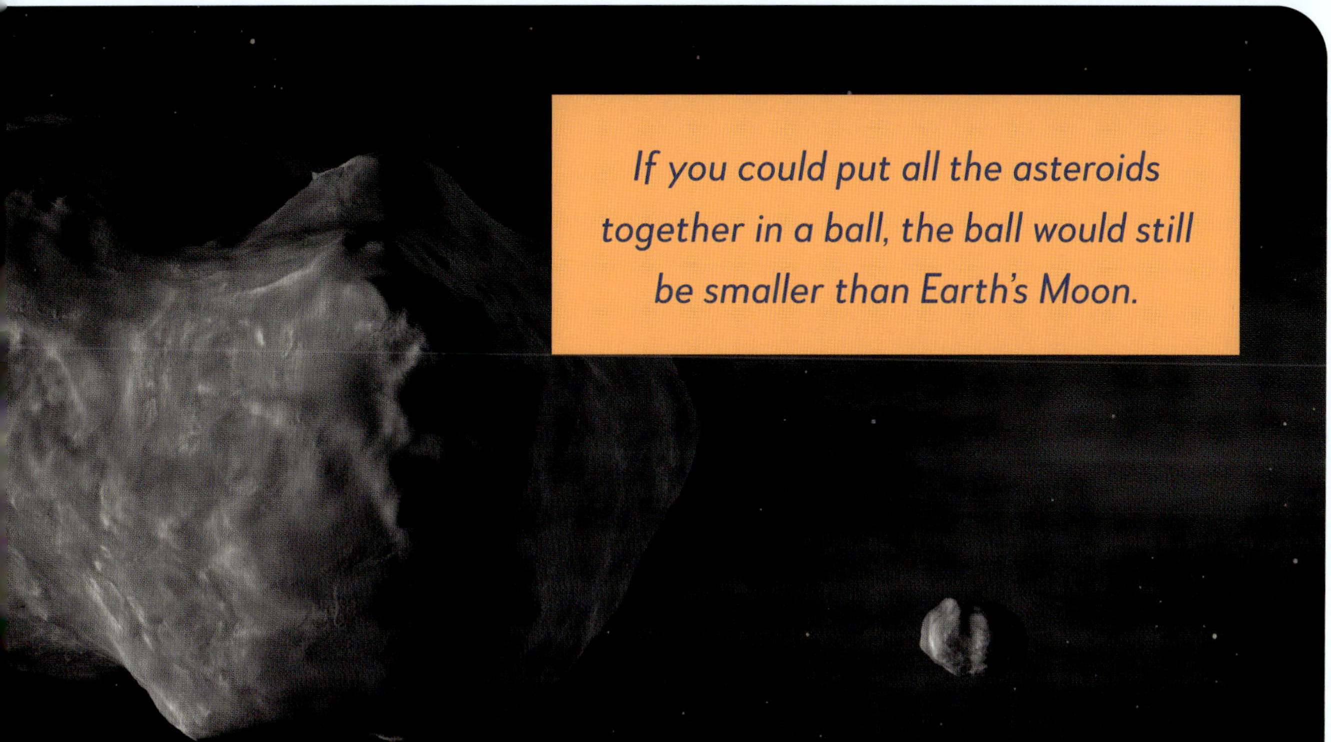

If you could put all the asteroids together in a ball, the ball would still be smaller than Earth's Moon.

The asteroid belt is between the four rocky, solid planets closer to the Sun and the four giant, gassy planets farther from the Sun.

Most asteroids are in the asteroid belt. But some asteroids move closer to the Sun.

Ceres might have old water volcanoes and liquid water deep under the surface.

Ceres

Ceres is the biggest asteroid in the asteroid belt. But it is much smaller than the Moon or the planets. 2,500 Ceres could fit inside Earth.

Ceres is also a **dwarf planet**. A dwarf planet is like a small planet. Planets can't have other similar-sized objects near their orbits. But dwarf planets can! Ceres has other asteroids in its orbit. We'll talk about other dwarf planets later in this book.

Jupiter

Jupiter is the fifth planet from the Sun. It is the biggest planet in our solar system—all the other planets could fit inside it!

Jupiter is one of the four giant planets. It is made mostly of gas.

Jupiter looks colorful and striped. Those stripes are actually clouds and huge storms. The Great Red Spot is the biggest storm. It is like a giant hurricane that has lasted for hundreds of years.

Jupiter has 4 big moons and lots of small moons. Jupiter's moon Ganymede is the largest moon in the solar system. It is bigger than Mercury.

Jupiter and its moons are very cold. As we go farther from the Sun, it gets even colder.

How Big? Huge! More than 1,300 Earths could fit inside Jupiter

How Far from the Sun? About 5 Earth-to-Sun distances

How Many Moons? 79 discovered so far

Saturn

Saturn is the sixth planet from the Sun. It is mostly made of gas.

Saturn has beautiful rings around it. What are the rings made of? Dirty snowballs! Some are as small as a snowflake. Some are bigger than a school bus.

Saturn's moon Titan is the second-largest moon in the solar system. It is bigger than the planet Mercury.

In the night sky, Saturn looks like a bright yellow star.

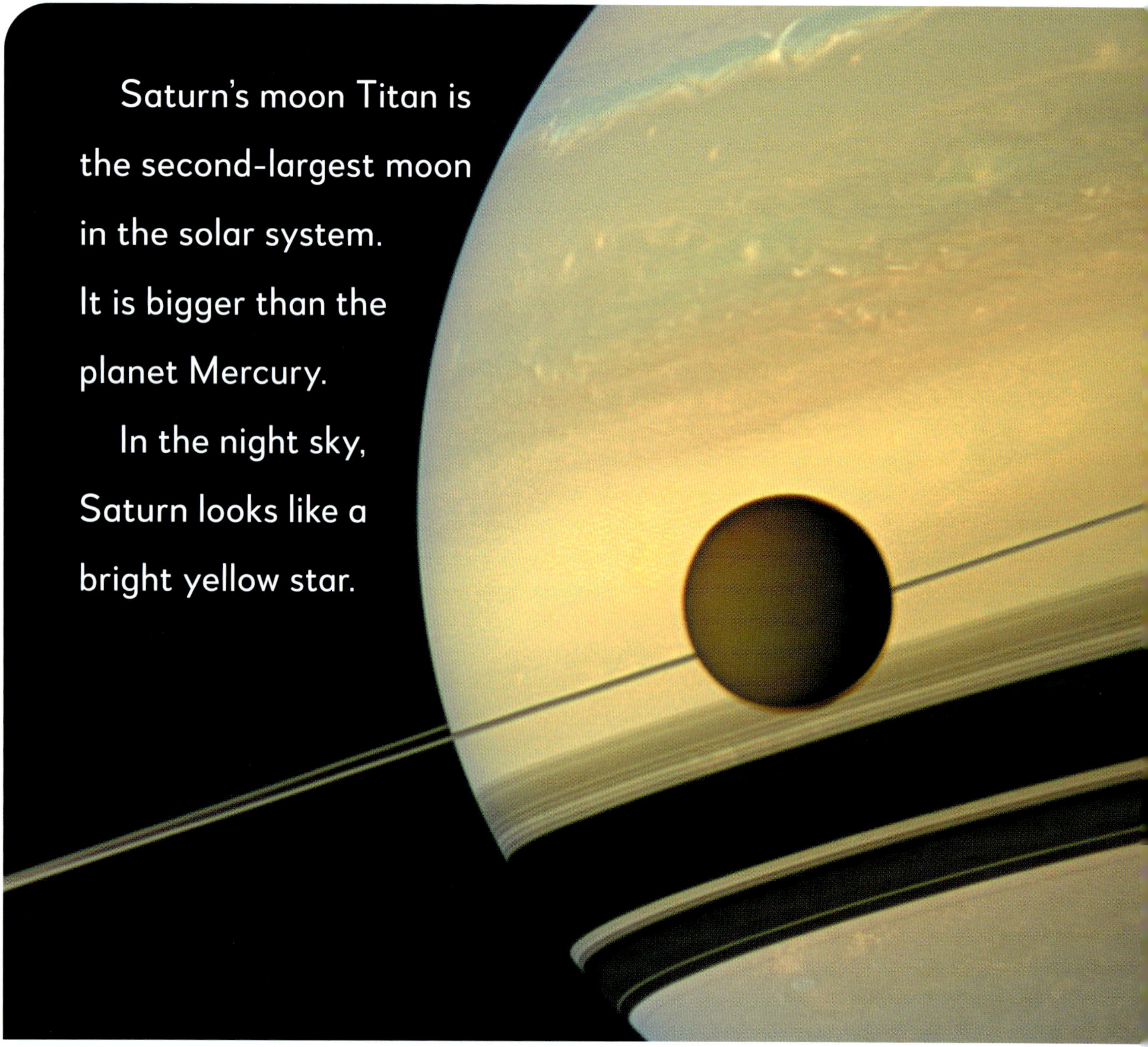

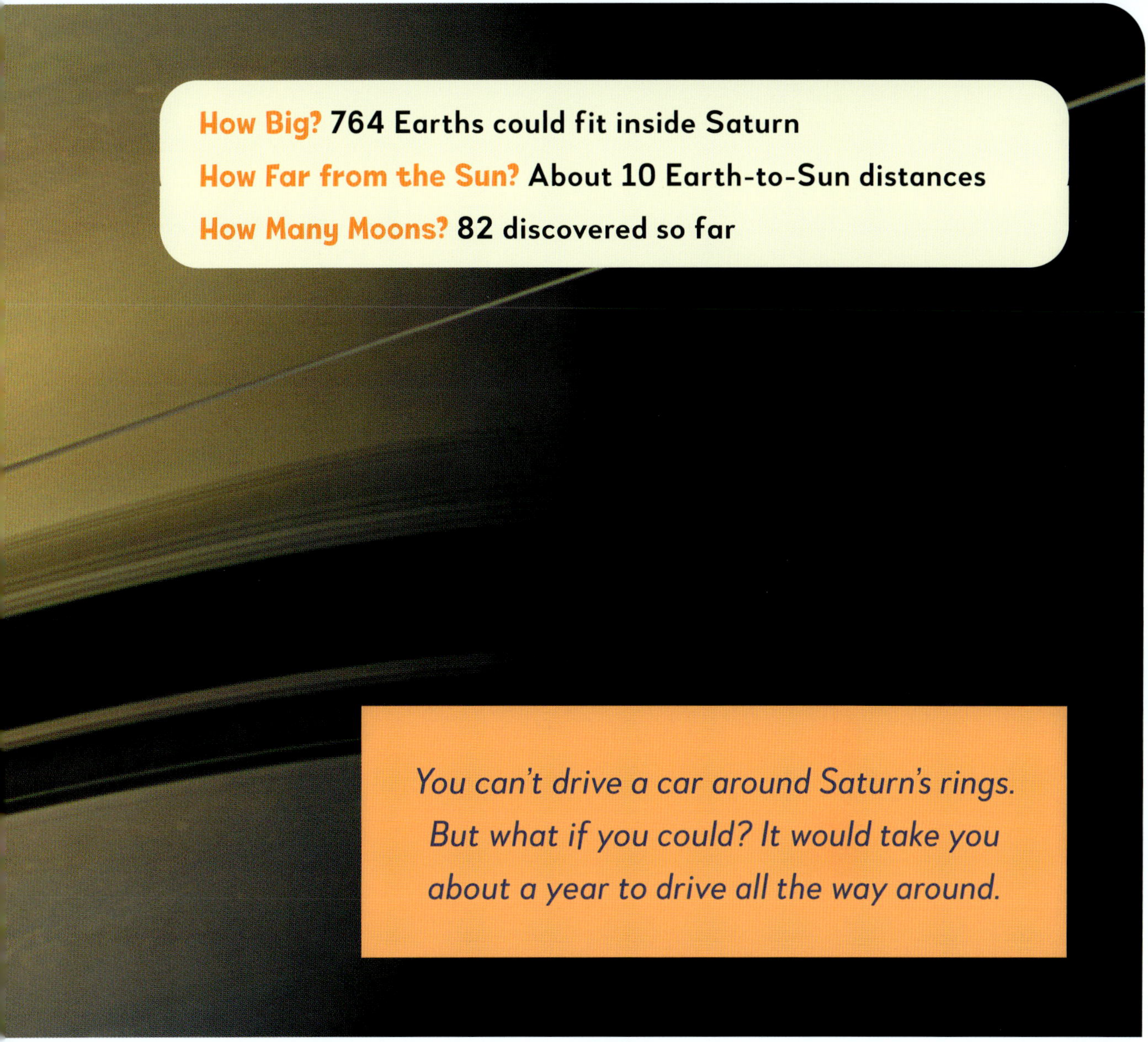

How Big? 764 Earths could fit inside Saturn

How Far from the Sun? About 10 Earth-to-Sun distances

How Many Moons? 82 discovered so far

You can't drive a car around Saturn's rings. But what if you could? It would take you about a year to drive all the way around.

Uranus

Uranus is the seventh planet from the Sun. It is a giant planet with lots of gas. You could not stand on Uranus.

Uranus is blue. It is tilted on its side compared to the other planets.

Uranus has a set of 13 mostly dark rings. They are hard to see, unlike Saturn's rings.

Each season on Uranus lasts 21 Earth years. Can you imagine 21 years of winter?

If you are somewhere very, very dark, you might be able to see Uranus in the night sky with just your eyes. Usually you need to use a **telescope** to see it. A telescope is a tool that helps you see things that are far away.

Artist's drawing

How Big? 63 Earths could fit inside Uranus

How Far from the Sun? About 19 Earth-to-Sun distances

How Many Moons? 27 discovered so far

Neptune

Neptune is the eighth planet from the Sun. It is a giant planet with lots of gas.

Neptune is like Uranus in many ways. Neptune is just a little smaller than Uranus. Neptune and Uranus are also both giant planets that are blue.

Neptune has a few rings, but they are very hard to see.

Neptune is a windy planet. It has the fastest winds on any planet in the solar system.

Neptune has 14 moons, but they are all small except for Triton. Triton is covered in strange ices.

To see Neptune, you have to use a telescope. Neptune is too far to see with just your eyes.

How Big? 58 Earths could fit inside Neptune
How Far from the Sun? About 30 Earth-to-Sun distances
How Many Moons? 14 discovered so far

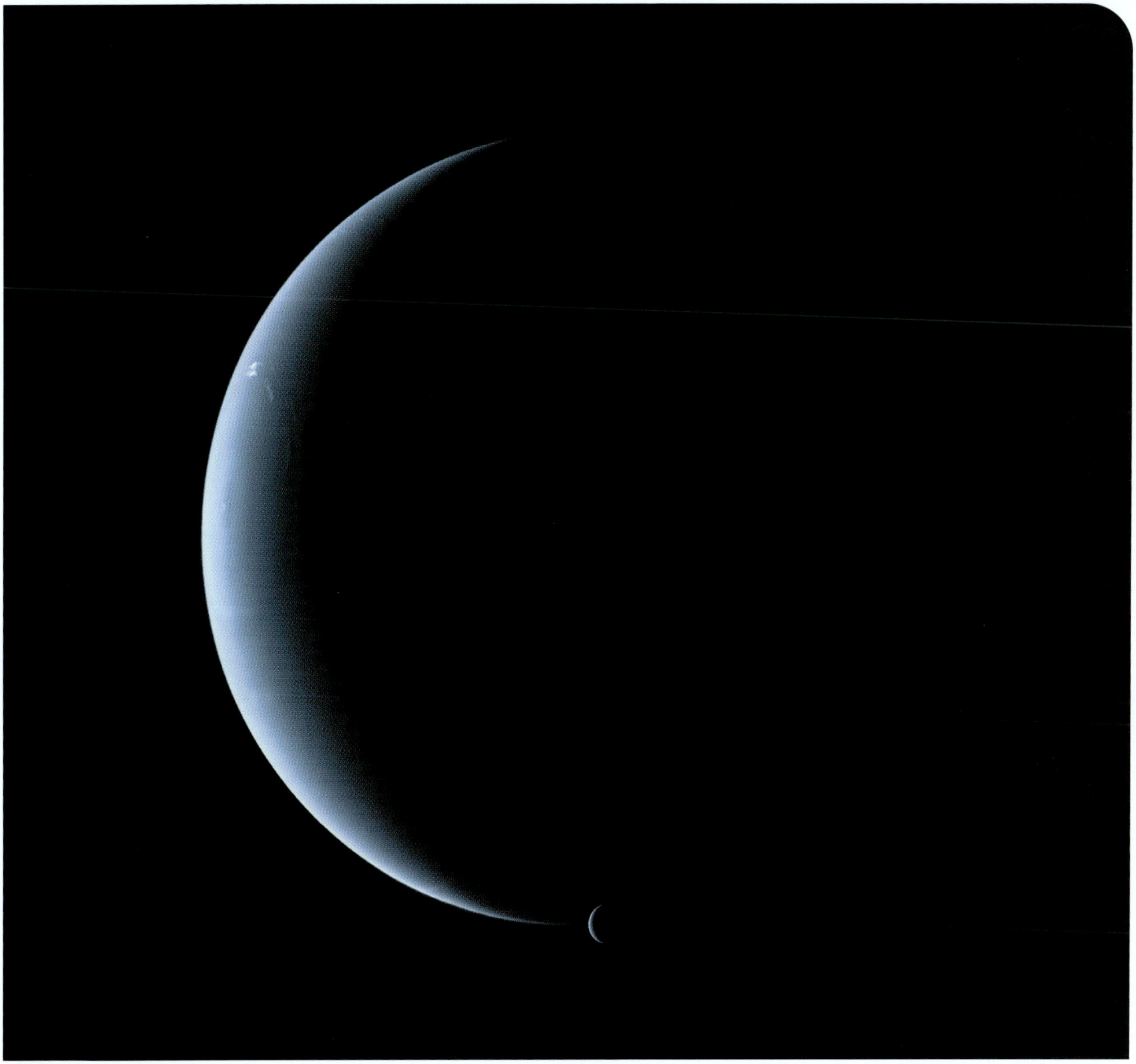

Beyond Neptune

There are objects beyond Neptune that also go around the Sun. Four of them are dwarf planets. They are named Pluto, Haumea, Makemake, and Eris.

There are also many things smaller than dwarf planets beyond Neptune. They are hard to find because they are so far away. But **astronomers** are looking and finding more things. Astronomers are people who study everything outside of Earth, like planets and stars.

Pluto
Eris
Haumea
Makemake
Artist's drawing

Pluto is smaller than Earth's Moon.

Pluto

Pluto is a dwarf planet that is usually farther from the Sun than Neptune. It is reddish. It is also very cold and covered in ice. It has a little atmosphere—in other words, it has a little gas surrounding it.

Pluto has five moons. Charon is the largest. Charon is about half as wide as Pluto.

Pluto is named after a Roman god. The name was suggested by an 11-year-old girl.

Artist's drawing of what Pluto looks like from Charon

Pluto used to be called a planet. But then astronomers found other objects the same size as Pluto. So they made up a new name, dwarf planet. Pluto and Eris are the largest known dwarf planets.

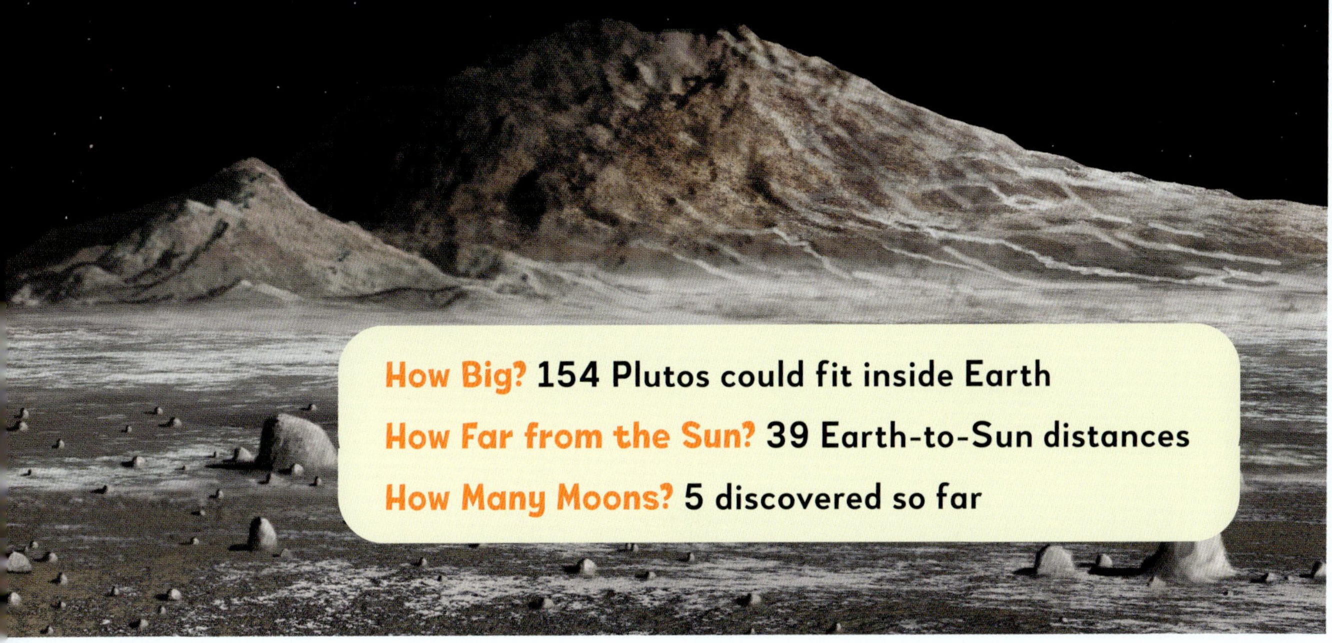

How Big? 154 Plutos could fit inside Earth

How Far from the Sun? 39 Earth-to-Sun distances

How Many Moons? 5 discovered so far

Haumea, Makemake and Eris

The dwarf planets Haumea, Makemake, and Eris are all far beyond Neptune and even Pluto. They are very far from the Sun, so they are extremely cold and covered in ice. They all have moons.

Haumea is weird. It spins very fast and is shaped kind of like a football.

Haumea is the only dwarf planet that we know has a ring.

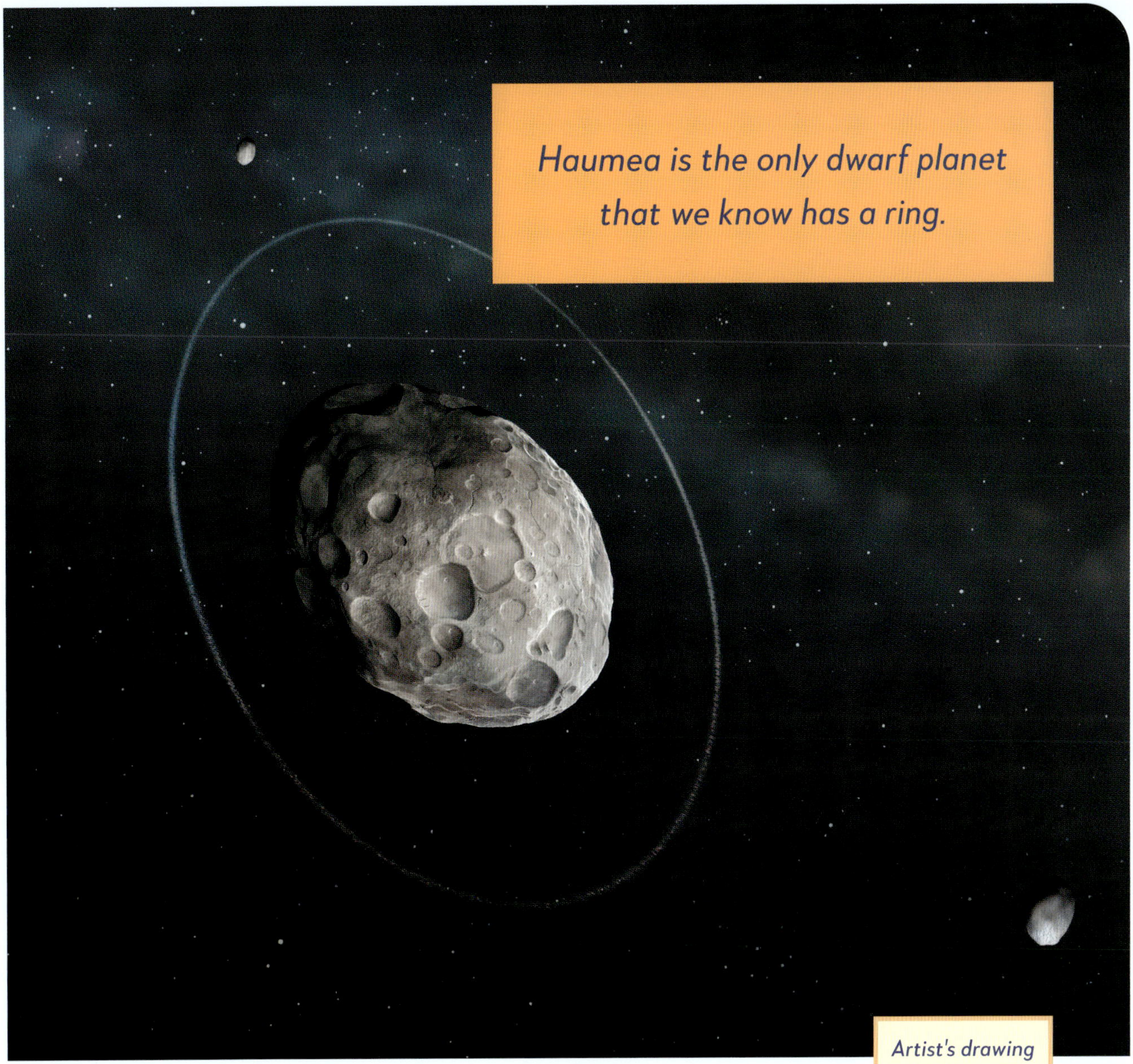

Artist's drawing

Makemake is smaller than Eris and Haumea.

It is reddish like Pluto.

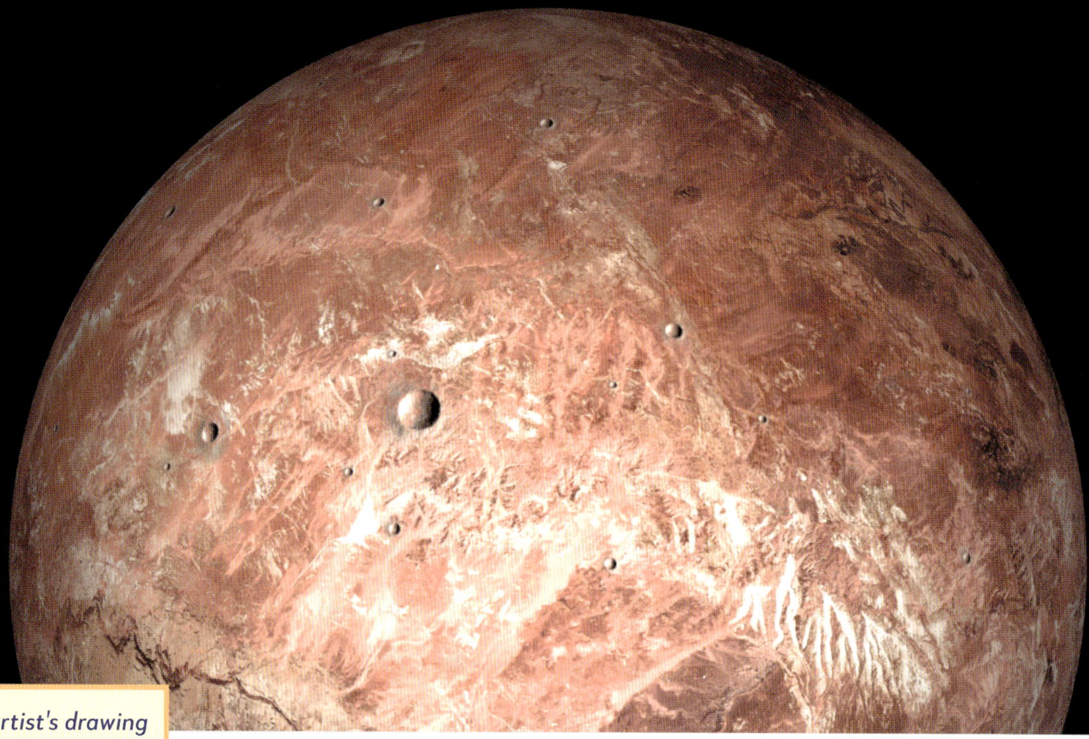

Artist's drawing

Eris is just a little smaller than Pluto. But Eris weighs more, so Eris probably has more rock and less ice than Pluto.

Scientists expect to discover more dwarf planets by using big telescopes.

Artist's drawing

Planets and You

This book is only the beginning. You can learn much more about planets and other exciting things in space. What would you like to learn more about?

Scientists also have a lot more to learn. Using spacecraft and big telescopes, scientists are studying the planets and learning more every day. Would you like to study planets when you grow up?

Keep learning and having fun with planets!

GLOSSARY

ASTEROID: A small natural object in space made of rock or metal.

ASTRONOMER: A person who studies everything outside of Earth.

ATMOSPHERE: The gases surrounding a planet, moon, or other object. Examples of gases are what you breathe and what fills balloons.

DAY: The time it takes a planet to spin around once. On Earth, one day is 24 hours.

DWARF PLANET: Dwarf planets are like small planets. A dwarf planet is a round object that goes around the Sun but does not go around another object. Unlike a planet, it has objects close to the same size near its orbit.

GAS: Something that isn't a solid or a liquid. Balloons are filled with gas. You breathe gases.

GIANT PLANET: A very large planet made mostly of gas. In our solar system, there are four giant planets: Jupiter, Saturn, Uranus, and Neptune.

IMPACT CRATERS: Bowl-shaped holes caused by space rocks hitting the ground at high speed.

MOON: An object in space that goes around a bigger object, such as a planet. Earth's moon is known as the Moon.

ORBIT: The path a planet, moon, or other object follows as it goes around another object. ("The Earth's orbit around the Sun is almost a circle.") Also, the act of going around another object. ("Earth orbits the Sun.")

PLANET: A big ball-shaped object that goes around the Sun but does not go around another object. A planet does not have anything close to the same size near its orbit. Including Earth, there are eight planets that go around the Sun.

SOLAR SYSTEM: The solar system has the Sun at the center and includes all the planets, dwarf planets, and other objects that go around the Sun.

SOLAR SYSTEM OBJECTS: Anything going around the Sun, including planets, dwarf planets, and asteroids.

SPACECRAFT: Vehicles that can travel outside of Earth.

STAR: An enormous ball of hot, glowing gas. The Sun is a star.

TELESCOPE: A tool that helps you see things that are far away.

YEAR: The time it takes a planet to go all the way around the Sun. One Earth year is about 365 days long.

ACKNOWLEDGMENTS

Thanks to Jennifer Vaughn for her guidance, love, and support, and to my sons, Daniel and Kevin Betts, for their support and for bringing happiness and fulfillment to my life. Thanks to my parents, Bert A. and Barbara Lang Betts, for supporting my interest in space. Thanks to Kathleen Reagan Betts for being such a great mom. And thanks to Bill Nye and the staff of the Planetary Society for their support of my broader education efforts. Thanks to Laura Bryn Sisson and Connie Santisteban for their editing, and to Joe Cho and the rest of the Callisto Media team.

ABOUT THE AUTHOR

Dr. Bruce Betts is a planetary scientist and children's book author who loves teaching people about planets, space, and the night sky in fun and entertaining ways. He is the author of *Astronomy for Kids: How to Explore Outer Space with Binoculars, a Telescope, or Just Your Eyes!*; *Super Cool Space Facts: A Fun, Fact-Filled Space Book for Kids*; and *V.R. Space Explorers: Titan's Black Cat*.

He has lots of college degrees, lots of big dogs, and two sons. He is the chief scientist and LightSail program manager for the world's largest space interest group, The Planetary Society. He has a BS and an MS from Stanford and a planetary science PhD from Caltech. His research at Caltech and at the Planetary Science Institute focused on infrared studies of planetary surfaces. He managed planetary instrument development programs at NASA headquarters.

Follow him on Twitter @RandomSpaceFact and facebook.com/DrBruceBetts, or check out his website, RandomSpaceFact.com.

IMAGE CREDITS

Cigdem Simse/Alamy, p. iv; Alexander Aldatov/Alamy, pp 2,3; RooM the Agency/Alamy, pp. 5, 58; vector-map/iStock, p. 7; NASA, pp. 8, 14, 15, 16, 18, 23, 27, 30, 33, 35, 36, 44, 50; Dennis Hallinan/Alamy, p. 11; World History Archive/Alamy, p. 13; IStock/iStock, p. 19; Allexxandar/Alamy Stock Photo, pp 20/21; Susan E. Degginger/Alamy, p. 22; Martin/Alamy, p. 24; World History Archive/Alamy, p. 26; European Southern Observatory/Science Source, p 28; World History Archive/Alamy Stock Photo, p. 38; NASA/ESA, L. Sromovsky (UW-Madison)/H. Hammel (SSI)/K. Raes (SETI)/Science Source, p. 41; Alamy, pp . 42, 43; Worldspec/NASA/Alamy, p. 47; Meletios Verras/Shutterstock, p. 49; Mark Garlick/Science Source, pp. 52, 53, 55; Martin/Alamy, p. 57; Author photo courtesy Jennifer Vaughn